Going Solo
Creating your freelance editorial
business

SfEP Guides

The SfEP Guides series is intended for editors and proofreaders, both practising and potential, and other people involved in producing information, whether in the formal or informal sectors. The authors are usually senior members of the SfEP, and publications in the series focus on the core disciplines of editing and proofreading, while also extending occasionally into related fields such as writing, project management and web editing.

Other Guides in the series are:

Editing Fiction: A short introduction, by Imogen Olsen

Editing into Plain Language: Working for non-publishers, by Sarah Carr

Editor and Client: Building a professional relationship, 2nd edition, by Anne Waddingham

Marketing Yourself: Cost-effective ways to market your editorial business, 2nd edition, by Sara Hulse

Pricing a Project: How to prepare a professional quotation, by Melanie Thompson

Theses and Dissertations: Checking the language, by Pat Baxter

Your House Style: Styling your words for maximum impact, 2nd edition, by Christina Thomas

Going Solo

Creating your freelance editorial business

Sue Littleford

society for editors and proofreaders   s*f*ep

Published by the Society for Editors and Proofreaders
Apsley House
176 Upper Richmond Road
London SW15 2SH

www.sfep.org.uk

© Sue Littleford 2016

ISBN 978-0-9931293-1-5

The right of Sue Littleford to be identified as the author of this work has been asserted by her in accordance with the Copyright, Designs and Patents Act 1988.

The information contained in this work is accurate and current to the best of the author's knowledge. The author and publisher, however, make no guarantee as to, and assume no responsibility for, the correctness, sufficiency or completeness of such information or recommendation..

Editor: Gillian Clarke

Designed and typeset by Helius

Printed in the UK by The Printing Room, London

Contents

Introduction

If you're thinking about going solo with your own editorial business, or have recently got going, this Guide will help you steer through the things you'll need to consider as you set up your enterprise. As space is limited, there are lots of references to websites and other resources for you to gain fuller information. The booklet is heavily oriented towards the situation in the UK; readers in other countries will need to find out the appropriate business, legal and tax arrangements required for their own location.

As everyone will have reached this point in their career in their own way, guidance can only be general. You may need to take advice on money matters, for example, tailored to your current circumstances. Tax is dictated not just by your new freelance business, but by *all* your sources of income and your personal circumstances.

This Guide focuses on running your business. It assumes that you have already trained, or that you are taking care of obtaining the training you need, but I strongly recommend that you do train, although this Guide can't, for reasons of space, go into detail on what to train in and where to source it. Check the SfEP website if you're looking for direction on this.

A big thank you to the SfEP members who contributed their advice. Sadly there wasn't room to quote all of it. An equally big thank you to the reviewers – Helen Stevens and Alison Oakes – and to publications director Steve Hammatt, who steered this guide through to fruition.

1 Basics

Business planning

> *Create a business plan (including especially a marketing strategy) well ahead of time. There's little point in setting up a new business if you haven't worked out what services you will offer and to whom, and how you will enable your potential clients to find you and hire you.*
>
> Louise Harnby

You've either reached the decision to go into business for yourself or are thinking about it. I'm going to assume that you have, or are in the process of acquiring, a good grasp of editorial skills. So – what services will you offer? And to whom? The great thing about being freelance is that *you* choose. If you have a publishing background, you'll be able to use your contacts to find work, and will have a track record in a particular publishing niche that you can point to in your CV. If you're new to the publishing world – the second-careerists and similar – you may have skills from your old job that you can reapply in your own business.

Everyone, though, needs to think through a business plan.[1] And make no mistake, you're a business owner with obligations that HM Revenue and Customs (HMRC) will expect you to understand. So, in developing your plan, you will work out for whom you want to work, what you want to do for them, how you're going to abide by the law, how you're going to establish yourself in your new career and how you're going to look after your own well-being while doing so.

What services will you offer?

Are you a copy-editor? A proofreader? A developmental editor? Two of these? All three? Have you been a project manager? Do you also index? Do you already have a publishing niche? Do you have any prior expertise? Were you in medicine or in law, or were you a teacher or an academic? Do you want to continue to use that expertise, or are you looking for a complete break? In a sweeping oversimplification, people with some distinct expertise will find work more readily in that field and may well find it pays better.

Are you a specialist or a generalist?

Is your specialism by subject matter or by skill? What kind of demand is there for your specialism? What kind of competition is there from people offering similar skills and knowledge? Do you get bored working in one area all the time? Would you blossom chopping and changing between varied subject matter and exercising different skills? Some editors and proofreaders work in a specific subject area or for a particular type of client. Others have a range of skills that they use in a variety of spheres. It will help you to plan if you think about how you would like to work.

Can you apply previous experience?

No matter your starting point, you will have experience already that you can apply to your new business. You may be new as a business owner, but you may have a background in customer service, time management, negotiating or estimating, or you may have IT or subject-matter expertise. You may, indeed, have a publishing background! Draw on your past to inform how you run your business and to identify editorial niches that you would like to occupy, where you may have an edge over other editors and therefore capture the work.

Who is your client?

Once you know what services you will offer through your new business, you can begin to work out who your clients are. There are three broad areas:

- Businesses: If your background is in business, marketing or finance, you may want to work with businesses on annual reports, marketing materials and so on.
- Publishers: Work with publishers is getting harder to find, with takeovers, downsizing, outsourcing and the current move to oblige the authors to have their work edited, but it's still available.
- Authors: Many editorial professionals choose to work directly with authors where there is demand, but perhaps less understanding of what editorial help is available and how to choose it wisely.

The internet is awash with advice that authors don't need editing, or that their friends will do it free of charge. However, with Amazon taking an increasingly firm line on the technical quality of self-published works on their platform, there may be some rebound yet to come in favour of professional editing.

Think all this through. Your answers to the four questions listed above will dictate how you market yourself and where you will search for clients.

Branding

You've decided what services you're going to offer, and to whom. So how are you going to convey that in your branding – the way you present your business to the world at large and potential clients in particular? Decisions include choosing a name for your business, a strapline, a logo, your corporate colour scheme.

The name you trade under should be simple to remember, distinctive, describe the services you offer (or at least not make them a surprise!) and, ideally, not used by anyone else. Check your shortlist of potential names on the internet, to see if you're sufficiently distinctive not to lose business to an established enterprise in the same field, and with a domain name registrar to see if you're likely to be able to register a domain name that makes sense with your trading name.

Some people support using your own name in your business name whereas others prefer to go for something more catchy and corporate-sounding. If you know your name is one people struggle to spell correctly, something shorter and/or simpler may be the way to go.

You'll want a logo to use on your website, your invoices and so on. You may be able to design something yourself, or you may prefer to hire someone who can show you a range of designs and then provide files in the range of formats you'll need for different uses. I had my logo made for me, and produced in colour and as a black & white file. I use the black & white one for documents for printing so the logo comes across crisply. If you choose to hire someone, do think first about the image you want to project, the message you want to get across and the kind of colours you want to use. A designer will thank you for giving them a brief to follow – they shouldn't be expected to guess what you might want! While you're thinking about your logo, give some thought, too, to the typeface you intend to use in your communications – it's all part of your branding, and the two should work in harmony.

Advertising and marketing

Now it's time to think about how you will get your name out there, in front of your preferred type of client for your preferred type of work.

Received wisdom states that advertising doesn't work for editorial professionals. I think that really depends on where you advertise, though. I picked up a major, long-term client when he was browsing the *Yellow Pages* looking for a local copy-editor. But you must be aware of your costs and the value for money your advertising budget is giving you. See Chapter 4 for more detail.

Budgeting and monitoring

Even if you're not yet operational, you will need to get a grasp on the money side of things. For some reason, a lot of freelances are shy about the money. Don't be. This isn't a hobby, it's your business – the way you're going to put a roof over your head and food on the table. Be cool, calm and businesslike from the outset.

You'll start incurring expenses before you land your first client, which HMRC refers to as 'pre-trading expenses'. You'll need to record what you spend, when and on what (for more on this, see Chapter 3) even though you're not yet open for business. Do exercise caution and buy only what you really need. Don't let your enthusiasm for your new enterprise see you buying every book on grammar and editing that you can find!

Starting a business from scratch is usually a long, slow haul. Some freelances will be established sooner than others; some established freelances will, sad to say, experience gaps in their workflow, and therefore their cash flow. Think through now how you will fund yourself if you struggle to find work. Lack of cash flow has brought down many more businesses than lack of profits.

Many find it beneficial, if they're currently in paid employment, to start building their business at weekends and in the evenings – very hard work, but it does mean that you're fed and housed while you get going. As more freelance work comes in, it may be possible to go part-time and only become a full-time freelance when you're confident that you have the client base to support you. How you cut over to being a freelance will dictate your budget, but received wisdom is that you should have at least half a year's salary in the bank before you go solo if you are to support yourself.

Marketing handouts

It's often useful to have something you can hand to a prospective client, that tells them more about you and what you do. Depending on your target market, this could be a leaflet or a CV. A leaflet allows you to say what you will do, and a CV what you have done. Both of these documents can also be placed on your website as PDF downloadables, to give your marketing materials greater reach.

Keep CVs short and up to date. Write a core CV that you can amend to suit the potential client that you're sending it to.

You don't need to include your age, or anything that gives away your age, such as the year you took your A levels. Don't clutter it up with personal information (e.g. marital status, number of children or hobbies) *unless* it's directly relevant to the client's needs in an editorial freelance.

Email it as a PDF so you have control over how it looks if it's printed out.

Keep your CV under review frequently for the first two or three years – the whole thing – as you learn what works and what doesn't. Put notes in your diary to remind you to do this review. Each time you revise it, do check it carefully (and have someone else read it closely). In this business, typos in your CV won't win you any clients.

See also 'Adapting your CV' in Chapter 4.

In a marketing leaflet, you have more room to pitch your skills to your target audience and explain what you can do for them. Perhaps they are businesses that may not have considered buying in editorial expertise before, or you want to reach students and academics. Before going to the expense of having the leaflet printed, do consider how you are going to get your leaflet into the hands of the people you're targeting. By mail? Putting them through local business's letterboxes? Leaving them in libraries and common rooms? This will also guide you on how many copies to have printed.

What do you need?

The computer

You will, of course, need a computer. Microsoft Word is the dominant program for editing. Proofreaders will need a PDF reader program. Start off with the free versions; you can upgrade to the paid ones, which are more feature-rich, if you find you need more to meet your clients' requirements. Copy-editors may well be expected to mark-up artwork on PDFs, so they, too, should have a PDF program. SfEP members tend to use Adobe Acrobat, Adobe Acrobat Reader DC and PDF-Xchange Editor.

In other chapters there are mentions of additional software. Explore these during this business planning phase so you have a shopping list for those you think you'll get good use from but have to pay for.

There is no clear winner between PCs and Macs for editorial work, but note that some programs you might want to use will work on a Mac only if you also run a program such as Parallels. Another option is to buy a cheap laptop to run PC-only programs such as PerfectIt.

If you've had an IT department at work to rely on, it may come as a shock to realise you're now solely responsible for IT security, backing-up data and having a disaster recovery plan so that, if your computer dies, your client's deadline doesn't. One of the greatest mistakes any freelance can make is being sloppy about security. It's not conducive to a good working relationship if you infect your client's computers with a virus carried on an email you've sent.

Plan a periodical housekeeping ritual to tidy up documents and emails into folders, and to delete (or back-up onto external media) those no longer needed so that you keep your computer well organised and you can find things easily. And organise your email and folders so that things are readily to hand. This includes planning naming strategies for work files. Some will be dictated by the client, but your working copies need to be well organised so that you know you're working on the right version.

There are people who like to work at a desk with a big computer and there are those who like to work on the sofa with a laptop, which they can also take out into their garden or to the local coffee shop and keep working.

Have as big a monitor as you can afford, or will fit on your desk. Many people recommend using two or even three monitors: you can keep reference material open on one and the document you're working on on the other. It's perfectly possible to work well with just the one. I use my iPad for reference material as I've not the room for a second monitor, but my 28-inch monitor lets me have two documents open side by side in Word at full size, and has enough room in the tray that I can have many documents and programs open without their thumbnails being stacked. People who have more than one monitor often recommend having the one with the document they're working on set up portrait style.

Laser printers are fast and cheap, and unless you have a particular need for colour printing, a black and white laser multifunction device (prints, photocopies, scans and may also fax) is a good choice. The ideal of a paperless office is just that – you may well end up printing things, regardless. Do check out the price of toner for your shortlist of models before making a final choice.

Broadband speed is critical, especially when using back-up facilities in the cloud or if you need to do a lot of fact-checking, where slow speeds will be frustrating. If a high-speed service is available in your area and you can afford to do it, I recommend upgrading to the faster speed.

Office environment and furniture

Working at the kitchen table is certainly possible, but not ideal; aim to have a space where you can leave your work undisturbed, and on which you can shut the door at the end of the working day. Have the most comfortable and supportive chair you can afford, a desk you can spread out on and a footrest if you need one (perhaps even one on which you can do exercise). See Chapter 5 for more information on ergonomics and preventing RSI.

You'll need somewhere to file finished jobs, at least for a while, and if your work generates paper, this will be more of a physical issue than if everything is backed-up in the cloud. Retention time will depend on your client's requirements. Some clients will insist that you delete files and destroy papers as soon as you return the completed work; otherwise, think about keeping jobs until publication, at least. Beyond that, you're now your own boss so take advantage and personalise your space as much as you like!

Stationery

With your logo file(s) you can make your own stationery. Explore Word's customisable templates for standard stationery items. You'll need at least an invoice, and perhaps an account statement if your business generates lots of smaller invoices to a client and you need to provide a monthly statement of what's been issued, what's been paid and what's outstanding. Business cards can be designed very easily and cheaply on the website of one of the many companies offering such services. These days it's probably not necessary to pay a printer for a stack of your letterheads and invoices, and compliments slips are pretty much redundant, so start small and if you feel the need to have professionally printed stationery (beyond business cards), fine – but don't spend the money until you've established the need.

Resource materials

You will need certain reference materials, depending on the work you plan to do, and a shortlist of the most important is given in Chapter 2, though your own specialism, if you have one, may well dictate additional essential reference works. You should also be aware of the wide range of style guides (again, see Chapter 2).

Website

A website is essential, unless you have a raft of industry contacts and an established reputation in publishing, with no need to advertise. Potential clients are sure to check you out online and a website gives you a chance to set out your stall, as well as give you a more solid, established feel. See Chapter 4 for more detail.

2 Knowledge

A successful business relies on competent staff (in this case, you). And your profit margin will depend in part on how efficient you are in carrying out the work. It therefore makes sense to be sure that you know your stuff, and to keep up to date. This is recognised by continuing professional development (CPD) being an allowable business expense for income tax purposes.

Training

Training comes in many forms, but some of the most recognised courses are those provided by the SfEP, The Publishing Training Centre, Publishing Scotland, Publishing Ireland, European Association of Science Editors (EASE) and Editorial Freelancers Association (EFA, in the USA). For members of the SfEP, training is essential to upgrade beyond Entry Level (or to join as an Intermediate Member or higher); for Advanced Professional Member level, evidence of CPD is required.

If you have had no formal training, even if you have learned on the job but particularly if you are self-taught, do begin with basic proofreading or copy-editing skills courses from reputable suppliers, to ensure that you have the nuts and bolts of your trade at your fingertips. Such training will correct any bad habits you may have picked up, fill in gaps in your knowledge you may not even have realised were there, and give confidence to clients that you know what you're doing. Classroom-based courses will also provide networking and social opportunities.

After you are solid in the basics, look for training to take your skills to a higher level, including branching out into specialist training according to your target market or interests. Learn the best techniques for efficient and effective working, advanced Word skills, InDesign, proofreading PDFs, handling references lists, dealing with heavily illustrated books, preparing files as e-books, editing websites and so on.

Training to keep you up to date is an allowable business expense; training to enable to you start trading, or to develop a *new* specialism is not.

SfEP mentoring scheme

SfEP members may wish to explore the opportunities offered for mentoring, with an experienced copy-editor or proofreader supporting your practice on real materials.[2] Mentoring is available for copy-editing and for proofreading, with subject specialisms offered for fiction, biomedical journals (copy-editing only), academic law and academic music (both for copy-editing and some proofreading). SfEP plans to extend this list, so check the website for the latest offerings. Mentees must have first completed relevant SfEP training courses satisfactorily, and pay a fee.

Mastering your tools

Almost all editing these days is done on-screen, and most proofreading is done on PDFs. There will be exceptions, of course, but the days of sitting quietly with a stack of paper are fading rapidly. This means that copy-editors should be ready to handle Word styles, templates, macros, wildcards and master documents, and for some jobs be able to work within clients' systems, which will require you to be reasonably computer-savvy and adaptable. The SfEP Macros forum is a great source of help. Proofreaders will want to be competent in marking up PDFs with stamps of the proofreading symbols or the program's built-in-tools, according to the client's requirements.

Be alert, too, to additional software that will improve your efficiency, help cut down on distractions, keep track of your working time, and run your accounts and invoicing (links for many examples of these are in Chapter 6). SfEP forums, local groups and Facebook groups are great places to ask about and discover the tools that others find useful. Take advantage of free trial periods to road-test different apps to see which work best for you, but do spend some time exploring the features; when you have made your choice, master the program so that you get the best out of it for the least effort. Time spent doing things the hard way is time that you could have spent earning money, being with family and friends, or just putting your feet up.

Reference books

There are more and more reference books available, of varying quality and usefulness, and more and more of them have online versions. The online versions can be very handy, but their usefulness pales if your internet connection goes down at a key moment.

You will need a range of dictionaries according to the languages and varieties of English you work in. Most publishers will specify the dictionary they want used. *Oxford Dictionaries Online* also gives you access to a variety of other resources, such as *New Hart's Rules* (*NHR*), *New Oxford Dictionary for Writers & Editors* (*NODWE*), *Garner's Dictionary of Legal Usage*, *Pocket Fowler's Modern English Usage*, but *not* the *Oxford English Dictionary* (*OED*). But give serious consideration to owning the physical copies as well of those you find you use most – probably *NHR* and *NODWE*. The *New Oxford Spelling Dictionary* (*NOSD*) is particularly useful for proofreaders as it shows where wordbreaks should fall.

The annual subscription to the online version of the actual *OED* is eye-watering for a freelance, so check out what your library card will do for you. Many local libraries will give you access to lots of Oxford and other resources free of charge and you can log into their websites using your library card number. The libraries page of your council's website may well list the resources available this way.

You may want your own copy of other books, including *Butcher's Copy-Editing* (now in its 4th edition, ed. Maureen Leach and Caroline Drake) and *Fowler's Dictionary of Modern English Usage* (ed. Jeremy Butterfield). *The Chicago Manual of Style* (*CMoS*, also online) is a mainstay for many who edit in US English, together with *Garner's Modern English Usage* (newly retitled from *Garner's Modern American Usage*). You may well have subject specialisms that need reference works, too. As you add to your collection, if you buy through Amazon you can give the SfEP a small commission (from Amazon's pocket, not yours), by making your purchases via a special link.[3] Look at editions of the SfEP's magazine *Editing Matters*[4] for reviews of new books in the editorial and language fields.

Check the Benefits section in the members' area of the SfEP website to see what discounts are available.

Style guides

It is informative and eye-opening to consider some of the many style guides commercially available. There is a (small) selection at the Wikipedia page on style guides[5] that you might explore, especially if your previous experience has been rather narrow.

And, of course, each publisher (and enlightened companies and organisations) will have their own style guide, such as the BBC, the UK government, and BuzzFeed,[6] which is interesting for its capture of current buzzwords. *Simplified Technical English*[7] is invaluable for those who edit in that field, as is *Scientific Style and Format*.[8]

Not all clients have a style guide. If you have to work one out for a job, Christina Thomas's SfEP Guide *Your House Style: Styling your words for maximum impact* has lots of helpful advice on what should be included in a house style. It also lists useful guidelines for websites and print material.

Social media

This is the time to embrace social media, if you've been holding back. It is an invaluable resource for getting advice, problem-solving and picking up tips on best practice. The SfEP forums are the first port of call for members. They cover the general forum SfEPLine, newbies, macros, a marketplace to find work passed on by other members, forums for each local group, fiction, ELT (English language teaching), education, legal, medSTEM (science/technical/engineering/medical, focusing on medical editing), working with non-publishers and more.

> *Join the forums and your local SfEP group if you have one. It's enormously helpful when you're just getting going to realise that you're not on your own, and you can get lots of great support and advice from colleagues – some of whom are in the same position as you, while others have been in the same position in the past.*
>
> *Steve Hammatt*

Facebook groups such as the Editors Association of Earth (EAE) and its associated groups are also fantastic places to check usage with native speakers of different Englishes. It's rare that you will work just in UK English, so if you want to see whether a phrase works in another English, these groups are great places to get a quick response. There are many editors' and proofreaders' groups on Facebook and LinkedIn, but do tread carefully and judge which ones are populated with people who will steer you in the right direction.

Do think about keeping your personal and professional presences online distinct. You may well want to create a Facebook page for your business and keep clients there, and have a separate Twitter account. If your online presence has been, er, vibrant, you may also want to think about culling posts so that you present only a professional aspect to potential clients.

If you are very new, joining groups on Facebook and/or LinkedIn, or following people and organisations on Twitter can be educational, even if you only lurk (read posts without writing any of your own).

Continuing professional development

The world of publishing, and the production of documents in other fields, is changing faster than ever. New tools, new norms, are developing all the time. Think about your CPD to ensure that you do not get left behind, and can stay competitive in what you are able to offer to your clients. When preparing your budgets, be sure to allocate some expenditure to CPD each year.

Less formal CPD can involve keeping abreast of publishing news, via channels such as *The Bookseller*,[9] the Publishing Perspectives website,[10] reading books and blogs related to your practice and interests, and participating in the SfEP forums[11] and local groups.[12] The *Copyeditors' Knowledge Base*[13] by Katharine O'Moore-Klopf is a great source of ideas for reading and CPD, as well as answering knotty questions.

3 Money

The importance of keeping track

Financial records fulfil very important functions. First, of course, you *must* comply with the requirements to keep track of income and expenditure for income tax and national insurance contributions (NICs) purposes. But beyond that, your records will tell you if you're profitable and if you're charging enough, whether clients have paid their invoices or you need to chase them up, and your records will provide an invaluable resource when it comes to pricing work (see Chapter 4).

What does your income need to cover?

Besides the outgoings you always had as an employee, your self-employment earnings have to cover your tax, national insurance, pension, sick pay, holiday pay and a cushion to keep you going if your cash flow hits a problem. Instead of income tax, NICs and pension[14,15] payments being taken at source by your employer, you will now need to budget for these. You will also want to make provision for times you can't or don't want to work, by saving for the equivalent of sick or holiday pay.

Income tax, national insurance and VAT

Your approach to your business is up to you. But whether it's something you're doing on the side for a little extra cash or to build up a client base ready to go solo, whether editorial work is something you do occasionally to keep yourself occupied or it's your sole means of support, HMRC will expect you to be businesslike about your finances and your obligations. It matters not a jot that you're a word person, and perhaps not a numbers one.

Record-keeping is a legal requirement. You will need to keep careful and accurate records of who has paid you, how much, what for and when. You will need to keep equally accurate and careful records of what you spend, when you spent it, what you spent it on and whether it was an allowable or non-allowable business or capital expense for tax relief purposes.

For your own sanity, it is best to keep these records as you go along. This will enable you to complete your tax return promptly, help to prevent receipts and invoices going astray and, if the government brings about its intention (announced in spring 2016) to introduce online updates of your financial position four times a year, you will be ready and able to comply.

What follows is based on straightforward circumstances in the UK. If yours aren't – you have other sources of income, you have employees or you are outside the UK – you should seek advice from HMRC direct (or your country's equivalent), or from an accountant.

Registering as self-employed

The gov.uk website explains how to decide if you're self-employed or not,[16] as freelance work can sometimes be treated as employment.

Note that it's possible to be treated by HMRC as an employee for one job (perhaps because of certain conditions from the client), but as self-employed on another. So you can be both employed and self-employed in the same tax year for doing the same kind of work. You can be hired to do a piece of work on terms that make you an employee in the eyes of HMRC, but that doesn't mean that you're not self-employed for other jobs you undertake.

If the terms of a contract make it impossible to justify self-employed status *for that piece of work* to HMRC, it may be that you should be treated as an employee, with tax, NICs and perhaps pension contributions taken at source under PAYE. Your employer will also have NICs and pension contributions to make on your employment and you will get a payslip for each pay period you were employed, with a P60 at the end of the tax year. You will need those for your tax return, where you will have to fill out both the self-employment and employee pages.

Assuming that you are self-employed for at least some of the work you're doing, you should register as self-employed *as soon as you make yourself available for work*, and in any event by 5 October of your business's second year (i.e. if you go solo any time between April 2016 and March 2017, you would need to register no later than 5 October 2017). The HMRC website guides you through the registration options and process[17,18] where there is a great deal of information for the newly self-employed. HMRC put a lot of effort into helping the self-employed get things right first time, and to pay the right amount in tax and NICs and on time. Less work for them, no penalties or interest for you.

Access to information about tax, national insurance and self-employment

Once you are registered, you can access even more information about the process. Subscribe to the HMRC Business Help and Education Emails service[19] to receive mailings that will keep you up to date with changes, and offer additional help and information for sole traders and small business owners.

Income tax

You will pay income tax on your *profits* each year, not your gross income, on the excess above your tax allowance. Your tax allowance will depend on your personal circumstances, but for someone with no dependants, spouse or disabilities, and uncomplicated tax affairs, it is £11,000 for 2016/17. One of the attractions of self-employment is that you can offset a great many necessary expenses against your income to reduce your taxable profits. Here's how it works:

Income	£17,500
Allowable business expenses	−£800
Taxable profit	£16,700
Tax allowance	−£11,000
Income tax payable on	£5,700

If you work from home, as a great many sole traders in the editorial world do, you can offset against your tax liability allowances for the use of your home for business purposes, including a proportion of heating, lighting, broadband and phone bills. HMRC introduced the simplified expenses scheme to save an awful lot of calculation and head-scratching, and sets out a figure you can claim each month on a sliding scale according to the number of hours worked (another reason to record these). You will need to decide whether you use this simplified scheme or work out your actual expenses (based on specific household bills and the space you use as an office); one method may be more beneficial than the other, but you won't know which until you have worked out the figures using both methods.

You can also claim professional memberships, such as the SfEP subscription, training costs of continuous professional development (but *not* training for a new specialism or to be in a position to start trading as an editor or proofreader, remember) with its associated travel (and, if it involves an overnight stay, subsistence) expenses, stationery and computer consumables, books, subscriptions to dictionaries and other resources, and so on. You can offset capital expenditure[20] – office furniture, computer hardware – against your tax liability, too.

For the detail of what you can claim, and what you can't, as allowable business expenses, the gov.uk website is the place to go, where you will find the *Self-employed Business Expenses* guide.[21]

You can claim for things bought prior to beginning trading that you need to start up your business – stationery, office furniture, equipment, consumables, advertising.

If you feel that the simplified expenses scheme doesn't work in your favour, you can still use the traditional expenses method. HMRC's videos and webinars, and the gov.uk website explain it all.[22,23]

Just as there are two business expenses schemes – traditional and simplified – for working from home, so there are two schemes for calculating the income on which you need to pay tax. The simplified scheme ('cash basis') means that you pay tax on income *received* during that year, unlike the traditional accounting system where the tax is calculated as at the date you raise the invoice. This means that you might be paying tax on income not yet received, indeed that you might never receive but write off as a bad debt (duly adjusted in the next tax return).

Deciding on your accounting year

HMRC recommends that the simplest business accounting year for calculating tax and NI liabilities is one that coincides with the tax year. You can reduce the length of your first accounting year to end on 5 April (or 31 March, if that's easier*). You can run your accounting year for a full twelve months from your start date if you prefer, but that will mean you have to split your data into two tax years each time.

You will be asked to state on your self-assessment tax return the date up to which your business accounts are made up (i.e. the end of your business accounting year).

National insurance

Class 2 NICs are being abolished from 2018; this whole area is in flux with proposals as to what will replace it, what voluntary arrangements may be needed to top-up NICs to ensure benefits and so on.

For now, Class 2 NICs are payable with your income tax. Class 4 NICs are payable on *profit* (not gross income). The sums due for NICs are calculated when you submit your self-assessment tax return.

Self-employed national insurance contribution rates 2016/17

Annual profits (£ a year)	Class 2 (£ per week)	Class 4 (%)
Below £5,965 (Small Profits Threshold)	0.00	0
£5,965 to £8,060 (Lower Profits Limit)	2.80	0
£8,060 to £43,000 (Upper Profits Limit)	2.80	9
Above £43,000	2.80	2

VAT

If your business is carried out solely in the UK, then, unless your turnover is more than £83,000 (April 2016 rate), you need not register for VAT *unless you want to*.

---

*Note that if you keep your accounts on a calendar monthly basis, you can treat 31 March as being the end of the tax year.

If you trade with overseas clients, you should check whether you are required to register for VAT. Lots more information can be found on the gov.uk website.[24,25]

Record-keeping for HMRC purposes

HMRC requires you to keep paper records of any document to do with tax – P45, P60, payslips, taxed interest statements from your bank, etc. – but receipts and invoices can be scanned. If you scan, check the quality of the image before ditching the paper copy, and make sure you scan both sides if something's written on the back.

You may find it helpful to organise your expenditure records by the categories HMRC uses, but if your takings are under £82,000 (2016), you can just provide a single total figure on the return. See page 2 of the long-form tax return for the list of categories.[26]

You must keep all your financial records for the current and the six previous full tax years.

If your records are destroyed, HMRC will expect you to try to reconstruct them as best you can. Advise HMRC if you have to do this. It will make your life easier if you scan even those documents you *must* keep as paper, and back-up the scanned images off-site.

Your first year in business – a warning about a bigger tax bill!

Although your tax is calculated on the figures for the tax year just ended, if the tax due is over £1,000 HMRC will collect half of the anticipated tax (which they call 'payments on account') for the *next* year with the initial year's payment. This arrangement keeps rolling forwards, so you end up paying your tax partly in advance, partly in arrears. If your tax bill drops below £1,000, no payments on account will be required, but it will start up again when your tax bill rises above the threshold once more. It is therefore important to think about budgeting for your likely tax bill – rather than just the tax on this year's earnings – and set money aside for tax and NICs from each payment that comes in.

HMRC has a tool[27] to help you work out your likely tax and NIC bill, so you can budget for it as early as possible. Note that the tool works only if you have very simple tax affairs, and no other income.

The advantages of completing your tax return as early as possible

Personally, I complete my tax return as soon as possible, then pay my bill in monthly instalments, mimicking PAYE. While interest rates remain so low, I may as well keep my tax bill under control. Other people prefer to keep the money in a savings account and pay at the very last moment, which is fine if you have the money ready. If you struggle to budget, consider making payments on account, during the year. You can even do this in advance of completing your first self-employed tax return.

Invoicing and chasing late payment

Invoices must include certain information by law[28] and it is a good idea to include on your invoice the date by which payment is due and that you reserve the right to charge interest for late payment (by another business; this law doesn't apply to private customers).[29] Then your client is in no doubt that you expect to be paid promptly and you have made your position clear from the outset.

You're running a business. Get your invoices out promptly and make it clear when payment is due. Record this. On the day after an invoice falls due, chase non-payment. I see too many forum posts saying how cringeworthy invoicing and pursuing payment is – asking people for money makes some editorial freelances' toes curl. Well, you just have to get past that. If you don't value your time and skill, who should? You're not asking for your pocket money. You're not asking for a favour. You are a business person who has delivered according to contract and the other half of that contract is payment for services rendered.

Record each contact regarding non-payment. Remain polite, but don't let the matter ride. Be businesslike and your client will (usually) respond in the same way.

Should you be a company?

Some freelances – even sole traders – have set themselves up as companies. There is more involved in that decision than this guide can cover, and there are tax and legal implications.

Do you see yourself as working alone and accepting only work that you know you will carry out yourself? Do you see yourself instead as being the focal point of getting work in, but employing others to provide at least some of the services? Is your market a high-risk one or one that expects to deal with organisations rather than individuals? It's probable that registering your business as a company from the outset is unnecessarily expensive and complex, but, depending on your ambitions, it may be something you should read up on and prepare for.

Do you need an accountant?

I'm afraid that there's no simple answer! A great many people do perfectly well without one. You may, though. find it worthwhile to employ an accountant for the first year or two to help you form good habits and to get advice on things such as business expenses. You may find it rather more worthwhile to use an accountant every year if your tax affairs are in any way complex. Accountancy fees are an allowable business expense.

Bank accounts

It's not necessary to have a separate business bank account, in the UK. You may find it easier to have one, though, especially if you have lots of smaller jobs, so lots of payments. Otherwise be sure to mark on your personal bank statements all income and outgoings related to your business.

If you are going to be working with overseas clients, you might need an account that allows you to accept payment in other currencies. This is worth considering when choosing a bank account.

You can offer other payment methods to your clients, in addition to cheques and bank transfers. PayPal is a popular choice as it allows clients to use a debit or credit card, although there are transaction fees to pay.[30]

4 Clients

Finding work

This is probably the single most daunting aspect of going solo.

No one can guarantee you work. You must go out and find it. Where you pitch yourself will depend on your chosen niche.

If you already have any contacts at all in the area you want to work in (former employer, friend-of-a-friend), use them.

If you want to work for publishers, a good starting point is the *Writers' and Artists' Yearbook* (either a physical copy, or the online version[31]), which contains listings of UK publishers, what they publish and their contact information. Search through, marking those publishers you intend to approach. Contact the switchboard to get the name and job title of the person responsible for editorial freelances; write or email, including your CV tailored towards that particular client (i.e. stressing relevant experience or knowledge useful to that client). You could also search www.yell.com under 'Publishers and Publications'.

Don't phone – you don't know that the person has time to talk to you there and then; they may well not note down your information, and they have nothing to refer to later. One thing you can say of all publishers is that they're very busy and they don't want their day sent off track by cold callers.

Keep plugging away at those enquiries to potential clients (keeping a record of approaches and responses) and do any proofreading/copy-editing test going.

Krysia Johnson

If you want to work with businesses, take a similar approach. Browse online for businesses that you're interested in, and find out whom to approach.

Target those who publish (be it publishers, self-publishers, companies, etc.) in your area of expertise, be it geography, knitting, law, or computer programming. Potential clients are far more likely to want to take a chance with a newbie with area expertise than with one without. And make sure you keep a careful list of those who you contact, and follow up each communication.

Janet MacMillan

You may find it easier to get work with book-packagers – project management companies that handle the prepress phases of copy-editing, typesetting and proofreading for publishers. They can be harder to track down, though. I've found one listed on yell.com under 'Printers and Lithographers', one under 'Advertising and Graphic Designers', one under 'Publishers and Publications' and I know a fourth that isn't in the *Yellow Pages* at all.

If your interest is in academic journals, you need to contact the publishers of the journals, again searching online.

In all cases, do take the trouble to find out exactly whom you should approach – if you can't find out via websites, phone the organisation and ask. And then make sure you spell the person's name and job title correctly!

SfEP members can join the Marketplace forum, where other members post job offers they can't take on, and there is also the Editors Association of Earth's (EAE) Ad Space on Facebook where job offers are posted, and people can say that they're looking for work.

Marketing and advertising

You can also advertise and wait for the work to come to you. Professional and Advanced Professional Members of the SfEP can take out an entry in the directory;[32] Intermediate Members (IM) can list themselves in IM Available.[33]

Thomson Local, *Yell* and other directories offer free entries. Or you can buy an entry in Yell.com, for example, which you can personalise with keywords and a description of your services, and which will link to your website. Check to see if your local authority runs a business directory.

Sara Hulse's SfEP Guide *Marketing Yourself: Strategies to promote your editorial business* contains many cost-effective marketing ideas, as does Louise Harnby's *Marketing Your Editing & Proofreading Business*.

Online companies offering all kinds of editing and proofreading are proliferating, most emphasising an incredibly fast turnaround time and zero 'errors' in the material after it's been worked on. Aside from the pressures that puts on the editorial professionals, it also raises unrealistic expectations in the public's minds; we all know that there is a variety of ways English can be used to express an idea, that spelling is, in some cases, a preference and that the correct use of the comma, the semicolon and so on is a matter of opinion and what-you're-used-to. Still, if you need to get a foot in the door, you could investigate these and sign up with agencies. Be wary of the ones that expect money from you upfront. They should be making their profit in the margin between what they charge the customer and what they pay you. Some are perfectly reputable, though, and indeed SfEP members get a cut-price deal with Freelancers in the UK.[34] So do your homework and you may find this a fruitful route to work.

Should you work for nothing, or for peanuts, just to get going?

When you're desperate for a job – any job – so you can start building a CV, it's tempting to work for nothing (or 'for the exposure' as many optimistic would-be clients put it. Well, just ask yourself how many famous editors you can name …). By all means volunteer your time to an organisation close to your heart, but think extremely carefully about doing unpaid work. What does that tell the client about how you value the service you offer? A quid pro quo, however, is quite different.

I know of an SfEP Professional Member who traded work for training when she first went solo: 'I did some voluntary work for a creative writing school, which was run as a charity. I learned a lot from the CEO and gained lots of experience. I also got my first two paid proofreading jobs as a result.' She adds, 'the CEO was also an editor herself and in exchange for my time she taught me how to edit the writing courses and articles for the newsletter/blogs. [It's] worth stressing that I received tuition as a swap for giving up my time to help. That was probably the most beneficial part for me. Although I was working unpaid, I wasn't really working for nothing. The CEO also recommended me to an author to proofread two of her novels.'

Networking

Network, network, network, online and in person. This will provide valuable info and contacts. It will also help you keep your sanity.

Sabine Citron

Networking is essential for your business at some level. If you are looking to work for businesses, you may join your local chamber of commerce[35] and go to events, armed with your business cards.

Use social media – some people find work directly this way. Others use it as an additional way of making their presence known, so that potential clients can look for them and gain reassurance that they are a genuine, viable business. The most business-focused site is LinkedIn, which can serve as an online CV. Facebook and Twitter are also popular. Follow the organisations that form your target market, and engage in dialogue with them.

If you want to work with self-publishing authors, there are many writers' groups and networking websites, and agencies that aim to put editor/ proofreader and author together.

Some of these agencies are more reputable than others. Some encourage driving the price down to ridiculously low fees and you should approach these with open eyes, though they may be useful to gain some experience. SfEP members can use the forum search option to look for threads discussing such agencies, or start a new thread to get a view on whether a particular agency is worth pursuing.[36]

Working for students

Many beginning editors consider working with students on theses and dissertations as a way of building up experience and getting an income. Whilst this is a lively market, be aware that there are ethical considerations. Each educational institution will have rules regarding what help a student may receive – references sections, for example, may be out of bounds – and you should ensure that the student is allowed to seek editorial help, and find out to what extent you may go in the edit. Pat Baxter's SfEP Guide *Theses and Dissertations: Checking the language* includes a discussion on setting parameters for your work and arranging payment.

Website

> *Personally I found that getting a website and getting it 'visible' online made a huge difference.*
>
> *Myriam Birch*

Your website will be as useful as you make it. Many clients will expect some sort of web presence from their potential editors and proofreaders, and it's usual for potential clients to check you out online. You can have a website built for you, but it is increasingly easy to build your own using WordPress (www.wordpress.com) or Weebly (www.weebly.com), for example. Search 'build your own website' online for many more providers.

If you register your own domain name,[37] you will be able to have businesslike email addresses which enhance your professional appearance, rather than one from your ISP or Gmail etc.

Include a clear description of what services you offer and how you can be contacted. You should explain your cookie policy and your privacy policy.[38] Take care to optimise your website's findability with good SEO (search engine optimisation) word choices, but don't go overboard with 'keyword stuffing' as browsers' algorithms may penalise you by dropping you down the results.

Consider adding a blog, if you think you have plenty to say on editorial matters, but be aware that you need to post regularly, if not frequently, as an unattended blog sends out the wrong message.

Also consider adding information useful to potential clients – advice, links – that demonstrates you understand your clients' needs and are a good match for them.

Adapting your CV

One size does *not* fit all when it comes to CVs. Keep it short. Two pages, good; one page, better; three or more pages, no. If you can't fit it all on one page, keep the most salient information on the front page – contact details, services offered, recent experience. Save effort by having a core CV that you then adapt for each client you send it to. Keep it classy, and lay it out clearly. This is your shopfront and you want to demonstrate to the client that you are up to the job. If you are sending your CV to a business, highlight your experience and knowledge of business matters and editing, and don't use up a paragraph on your fiction-editing experience. If you're sending it to a fiction publisher, don't have your non-fiction editing foremost.

Don't include any personal information unless it is *directly* relevant to your client. A keen sailor would want to mention that to a publisher of sailing books, for instance, whereas your fostering of children or of kittens would be relevant to different clients.

If you are sending your CV in hard copy, pop a business card in the envelope, too, loose, so that the recipient has two chances of finding your contact details if they keep business cards separate from their filing of A4 paper.

Keep your covering letter, or covering email, short and to the point. Introduce yourself, and say why you're approaching that potential client. Suggest why you're a good match for them, refer them to your accompanying CV for further information.

Pricing the work

The SfEP publishes suggested minimum rates per hour for proofreading, copy-editing, substantive editing/rewriting, project management and indexing.[39] A look at the SfEP's Rate for the Job resource,[40] though, shows the wide range of fees paid. It is clear there is no 'going rate' for editorial work in the UK.

Melanie Thompson's *Pricing a Project: How to prepare a professional quotation*, an SfEP Guide, is full of excellent guidance on how to work out what to charge in far greater breadth and detail than can be included in this booklet.

Remember that your fee must cover your time, your overheads and materials, your tax and NICs, your pension provision, your sick pay and your holiday pay (savings pots to help you over the rough times and the fun times) and leave you with a profit. That said, pricing yourself out of the market won't help.

> *Learn to put a high value on your time. It's not just about how much money you think your time is worth, it's about keeping enough time for yourself to enjoy doing other things, and not burning out.*
>
> Liz Jones

Rich Adin, a US editor, blogs frequently on pricing and other editorial business matters.[41] He has the American fixation on price per page that sounds odd to many UK editors, but he does make you think about your pricing covering making your living.

Record-keeping to help with pricing jobs

You will already be keeping records of invoices issued. Now add extra columns to your spreadsheet or record book to note the word count, type of work, type of job, hours spent, original estimate, and any complexities in the job (lots of tables or artwork, gazillions of footnotes or whatever applies to you). You will then build up a database to help price upcoming jobs, ensure that you're charging the right amount per hour or per thousand words, and have data to hand with which to negotiate with clients. Member Louise Harnby has shared the spreadsheet layout she uses, on her website.[42]

> *Keep full records from the very start (time taken, money earned, £/hour, £/1000 words, words/hour). This will enable you both to make more accurate estimates about cost and timing of projects and to monitor your own progress as these measures improve as you gain experience. It is really hard to generate these retrospectively.*
>
> Sue Browning

Negotiating price and timescale

> *When negotiating your fee, rate or whatever, state what you want and then shut up. If you can keep your nerve, you'll often find that your client will talk*

themselves into accepting what you want or close to it. After all, you've probably already established that you are available and have the skills required, and very few of those commissioning freelances do so with time to find alternatives. It is the urge to fill silences that makes many of us reduce our fees.

Nancy Duin

Increasingly, publishers and prepress services providers (aka book-packagers) quote a price for the job. Whether that price is what you want it to be is, of course, debatable and will vary from job to job and person to person.

Review the materials for the job as soon as they arrive, and check that you have everything. Then look through them and form a view on whether it's possible to do that job in the time allowed and for the fee offered.

If you consider that one or both of these are inadequate, you will need to go back to the client and state your case, negotiating for more time and/or money. Here is where your building database of jobs done and time taken/fee earned will be invaluable. You are a business, and you must take a businesslike approach to this, or you will find yourself working long, unsocial hours for peanuts and growing an ulcer, neither of which you bargained for when you decided to work for yourself.

Anne Waddingham's SfEP Guide *Editor and Client: Building a professional relationship* covers this area in depth and is full of useful advice.

If, on the other hand, you're asked to name your price, you will need to have in mind the bare minimum below which you will not go – the figure at which it would be a better use of your time to forgo this job and market yourself elsewhere. Also have in mind the price you would love to be paid for the job and start at that figure. If you can, get the client to state their budget first: you may be pleasantly surprised and thus paid better than you'd dare hope; or you may realise that there is no way you will come to terms, and save yourself the time and energy of negotiating on a job you cannot afford to take.

If you're asked to state how much time you need, programme in some wiggle room. How much will depend on the scale of the job, but your estimate of the date you will return the job to the client is *not* from how many hours the job itself will take, but how much time will elapse before it's completed. If you have commitments with your family, or another job, or you want to finish early one day, an eight-hour job may be finished in three days or a week. An 80-hour job may be finished in a month or six weeks. Or longer, or shorter, depending on what else is going on in your life.

Scheduling work

Schedule your life – all of it. Now that you are self-employed, your time is just your time.

Wendy Toole

There are many elements to scheduling, but the three main ones are:

- How many hours of work are needed for the job?
- What else am I doing at the same time?
- How much work can I do before my head explodes and quality goes down the drain?

Never, ever, *plan* to work at 100% capacity. What will you do if there is any kind of glitch? You get a tummy bug, the work is more involved than you thought, there's a storm and your power is cut? And if you routinely give 100%, what will you do when more is demanded? That way lie ulcers and meltdowns.

Taking on too much is not good for your health as I experienced recently, struggling through illness to complete an already stressful job with a too-short deadline.

Doreen Kruger

As a rule of thumb, you're unlikely to be effective for more than five hours of editing or proofreading per day. After that, fatigue will probably set in and your concentration will walk out of the door. If five hours seems short, note that it's considered that five hours' productivity is all that office-based employees can give each day, once you factor in time lost to conversations, meetings, phone calls, company (rather than task) emails and so on.

Aside from time working on editorial tasks, you will be marketing and networking, keeping your accounts up to date, reviewing your business and laying new plans, undertaking CPD and seeking ways to work more efficiently. All of these take time, and all of them are the first things to be jettisoned if you try to fit in too much editing or proofreading into your day. Yet as a business owner, you need to do *all* of this stuff yourself, now.

How you schedule depends on how you like to see your life set out, and whether you work on lots of short jobs with tight deadlines, or bigger jobs with longer deadlines and more wiggle room. You'll need some kind of scheduling help – a diary with *all* your commitments in it, whether online or on paper.

I usually work on book-length jobs, so client's schedules are generally a month, ish. I have clients booked loosely into slots a few months ahead. Each year I print a free A4 planner.[43] I mark each firmly scheduled job with a line of highlighter from the start date to the due date, which I label with the client and job name by writing along the highlighter line, and I literally pencil in those roughly reserved slots so I can see whom I need to inform as the start date becomes more defined, and whether or not I can take on an urgent, shorter job. This won't work for everyone, especially if you schedule in several jobs per day because you work on articles or marketing pieces or the like. In that case, an online diary would work much better.

> *Don't be afraid to say no to jobs. If you don't think you have time to do it, you won't. If you don't want to do it, don't. Whether you say yes or no, they may, or may not, ask you to work with them again. But if you say yes and do a poor job, it's unlikely they will ask you again.*
>
> *Julia Sandford-Cooke*

Sample edits and taking tests

If a publisher wants you to take a test to get into their freelance pool, take the test – but if it's a stupidly long test, you may not think it worth your while. After all, you're working for nothing while you're doing the test. Weigh up the pros and cons of taking a long test before completing it.

If an indie client (a business client or an individual) wants to see a sample edit, again, think about it first. Some editorial professionals make a point of offering a free sample on the grounds that it helps you gauge the amount of intervention the job needs, and it helps the client gauge whether you're the right editor or proofreader for them. There have, however, been instances of entrepreneurial individuals trying to get a range of editors to do sample edits of every chapter in their book, scoring what they see as a free edit and what we know will be a mishmash. Again, trust your instincts. Use the SfEP forum to see if anyone else has been approached.

If you want to offer free samples, be clear on how many words you will edit or proofread, and ask for a sample from the middle of the work; some would say

29

ask for bits from the start, middle and end. Received wisdom states that the first chapter or two of a book will have been worked on far more than the rest of it.

SfEP code of practice and client relations

The SfEP Code of Practice[44] is a source of excellent best-practice advice on the ethical running of your business and, by joining the Society, members sign up to observe it. There are additional documents available on the SfEP website advising freelances and clients on how to deal with each other.[45]

Contracts and terms & conditions

Some company clients will have a contract they will issue to you, setting out the responsibilities of both sides (you and the client). It's as well, though, to have your own set of terms & conditions (T&Cs) ready, that you can issue to clients in the absence of a contract (e.g. when working with individual authors). The SfEP has model T&Cs[46] in the members' area which may save you a lot of work in figuring out what to include.

Many publishers and prepress companies don't ask for a separate contract or signed T&Cs – an exchange of emails offering and accepting the work is binding. Increasingly, however, publishers require a contract (either one per job, or one that covers all jobs). Be aware that some of these standard contracts carelessly retain some clauses intended for corporate suppliers, or suppliers of very different services, that really don't apply to editorial freelances or that put unfair burdens on them. So read carefully any contract you are offered, and query or challenge any clauses that seem onerous – such as demanding indemnification for any losses, without an upper limit, or restricting for whom else you can work. It may take some determination to get the offending clause(s) struck out, but it is achievable much of the time. Give careful thought to going ahead with the job without a signed contract, though, in case things get sticky, and don't leave yourself exposed to working for nothing.

SfEP Professional and Advanced Professional Members can consult the legal helpline[47] regarding contracts they're unsure about.

T&Cs and contracts should protect both parties, spelling out what the work is, when it is due, what the fee is and when it will be paid, and what happens if something goes wrong, on either side.

If you work with individuals – authors, other small businesses – have your own T&Cs worked out and get the client to sign and return a copy. For individual clients, especially first-time clients, you may wish to request part (or all) of the payment for the work upfront, with the rest payable before delivery of the edited/proofread work. This information must be in your T&Cs.

Red flags and firing clients

It's important to not be afraid to say no. If the schedule isn't right, if the price isn't right, or if your gut just says 'I don't like this', it's best to say no. Something better almost always comes along instead, and it's better to spend time on marketing/websites/networking etc. than to work for pennies on a project that has you tearing your hair out and questioning what you've done with your life!

Kate Haigh

Some job offers may make you nervous. When you're trying to establish yourself in your new business, it's tempting to ignore those feelings and take the job and the money. But if you do, you may get more than you bargained for – a nightmare client, a nightmare schedule or an unpaid invoice. Trust your instincts. Some jobs are more trouble than they're worth.

One of the joys of freelancing is that you get to pick and choose your clients. If you don't want to work with someone, you don't have to. You can just say no. I see some editorial freelances tie themselves in knots giving reasons for turning the work down without hurting the client's feelings, or trying to fix the client up with another editor or proofreader. I've found the simplest approach is to say, as I did to one recent potential client, 'Thank you for contacting me, but I won't be quoting for this work. I wish you well in your search for an appropriate editor to work with. Many thanks for considering me.'

If you've taken on a client, and things go sour – perhaps they consistently pay late, so you have to chase up every invoice, perhaps they send promised work late, but won't move the deadline for return of the files, perhaps they have a new project manager you don't get on with – you can fire them. The next time they want to send you work, say no (if you don't want to burn your bridges with them, just say that you're fully booked), and go and find a client you like better. You don't have to do business with people you don't want to do business with. You're in charge of that.

5 You

Taking care of yourself

Working as a self-employed editorial professional can be hard on the body and on the mind. You may find yourself working for longer stretches of time without a break, or seeing other people far less often than you have been used to. It makes good sense to look after yourself as well as you can: you *are* your business.

The basic set-up: ergonomics and repetitive strain injury

You may well be spending longer at your desk for uninterrupted periods than you ever have before, and putting yourself at risk of RSI (repetitive strain injury). It's essential that you equip yourself with the best working environment that you can.

Take a look at recommendations for healthy arrangements of your office space.[48] Make sure you are sitting well, without straining eyes, neck, shoulders, arms or back. Denise Cowle, a physiotherapist-turned-editor, blogs on safe working.[49]

Your choice of mouse is also of great importance if you want to prevent carpal tunnel syndrome. Some people find it helps to switch the hand they use for the mouse (experiment with changing the button assignments if you do that). Investigate different shapes of mouse, including the baseball-shaped ones, vertical mice, stationary trackballs and pen-and-tablets.

It's now known that sitting for extended periods is injurious to your health, so it's important to take regular breaks from your work and get yourself moving. Standing desks are becoming more popular, but, if that's not for you, explore the world of seated exercise, with under-desk ellipticals and similar gizmos to keep your circulation going.

Some people work entirely on a laptop, but you can expand it and make yourself more comfortable – and work more safely – if you add on a mouse, a full-size keyboard and a larger monitor. You can get laptop stands that mean that you're not working looking down into the monitor, and the keyboard is on a slant.

See Chapter 6 for places to find ergonomic furniture and equipment.

Time management

It's essential that you keep track of how you spend your time, to improve efficiency, reduce stress and learn how long various tasks take you.

There are many facets to managing your time. You will need to record the time you spend working, for all the reasons previously discussed. You can track your time on a piece of paper, just writing down your starting and stopping times, then adding up the time spent. You may build a spreadsheet with the time marked into 5-, 10- or 15-minute blocks. And there are apps that will help you track your time for billing purposes. Many of these are listed in Chapter 6.

When it comes to looking at how you actually spend your time at your desk, you may find you need to force yourself to take breaks, or you may need to force yourself to work! Too many or too few breaks can create stress and other health problems. There are many apps to help, and several are listed in Chapter 6 for you to explore and see what works for you. Some will tell you when to take a break, some of them even suggesting exercises you can do; others will keep you away from social media, if you find that you're spending more time on Facebook than on the work you should be doing.

Do guard against working all the time. It's not healthy, and if you routinely work crazy hours, what will you do when there's some kind of crisis with a job or a client, or in your own life?

Support from others

If you find yourself working alone, as most editorial freelances do, take care to interact with people and set up support structures for your own sanity.

Some freelances like to work in shared workspaces, from popping into their local café once in a while to renting co-working space in offices designed to bring freelances together, to reduce feelings of isolation.[50,51]

Social media is a great place to chat with other editorial professionals. The SfEP forums and Facebook groups are perfect for this; they are also good sources of support and advice if you're unsure how to handle a situation with a client or potential client (taking care to preserve confidentiality). Less on-demand, but with the benefit of involving facetime with real people, are the SfEP local groups, local writers' groups and various networking events. The SfEP membership map[52] will help you find members in your vicinity.

Make time for friends and family, and think about how you schedule your work, so that you don't cut yourself off. Feeling part of a community and in touch with the world is one of the pillars of well-being.[53]

Planning for disaster

Disaster planning is like insurance – you hope you'll never need it, but you know you should have it. Just in case. Knowing that you have plans in place will reduce your stress levels at the most stressful time.

The most obvious disaster is your own ill-health at a crucial point in a job, or a persistent health problem that affects your ability to deliver to your clients. Your computer may also fail abruptly, or may be infected by malware. Other disasters include fire or flood affecting your home. Your office will also go up in smoke, or under the waters.

I'm prone to migraines, so I schedule two migraine days into every job. If you have a chronic issue, be realistic about how many hours you can work productively per day, and how many days per week.

Protect your computer with an antivirus program (yes, even if you have a Mac) and use it. Add one or, better, two, anti-malware programs, as no single program will find everything. But be aware that you may get performance issues if you load too many on your PC, or choose a pair that don't play nicely together. Set your firewall as tightly as you can that doesn't actually stop you from doing what you need.

Backing-up your work is critical. Consider cloud storage *with live back-up*. Popular ISPs such as BT offer a certain amount of storage free in their packages, with more available for a fee. Dropbox is also very popular. Backing-up files elsewhere than on your computer is essential if you are to recover quickly from a computer failure or infection. To back-up on your computer, set up Windows File History[54] or Apple Time Machine.[55] Back-up onto external media – hard drive or USB drive as you prefer, or as space demands. Back-up a recovery image of your computer twice and keep one copy off-site where you can access it easily should you need it; with a friend, perhaps.

Refresh a specific back-up of your browser settings and favourites, your contacts, to-do list, bookmarks, passwords and so on routinely, onto external media. If your computer dies and you need to replace it, being able to import all these features will get you up and running efficiently much more quickly than having to work it all out again.

Some people email files to themselves, so there's a copy on their ISP's server. Check that neither your settings nor your ISP's delete emails from the ISP's server as soon as they're delivered to your computer if you choose this route. It also doubles as a method of version control for documents.

Find a computer repair service *before* you need it – ask for recommendations, or at least collect more than one number – and store the details where you won't lose them.

If you can afford it, the luxury of a spare keyboard, mouse, monitor, computer and printer are great (as long as you still have access to your home, of course). Keep the spare computer updated if you don't want to be tearing your hair out when you finally switch it on and need to use it in an emergency.

Professional indemnity insurance

You should assess your risks and decide whether such insurance is right for you. At the time of writing, Policy Bee[56] is the SfEP's recommended insurer,[57] but others include Hiscox,[58] Caunce O'Hara[59] and Bluefin.[60] Some clients will require you to have professional indemnity insurance.

Upgrading SfEP membership and other goals

If you previously worked in an area where promotion was a possibility, and something to work towards, that disappears when you start to work for yourself.

One way to replicate – to some degree – the feeling of accomplishment that comes with a promotion is to work your way up the SfEP grades: Entry Level; Intermediate (at which point you can place an entry in IM [Intermediate Members] Available); Professional and Advanced Professional (which give you an entry in the directory and access to the legal helpline). All grades have the right to have an SfEP badge showing your grade on your website. The full list of membership benefits is on the SfEP website.[61]

Or set yourself other goals, perhaps joining networking groups. Take a look at the section 'Continuing professional development' in Chapter 2 for ideas to keep you focused and moving forward. Working for yourself gives you the freedom to build your business and your career in the way that suits you best, but it's also easy just to keep going at the same level, which can make you feel as if you're in a rut. Investing in yourself is directly investing in your business.

I hope that following the advice in this Guide will make it easier for you to navigate the many things you have to think about when going solo, and help get you up and running smoothly as you embark on this new phase of your career. I wish you good luck!

6 Resources

All URLs are correct as at summer 2016.

Business planning

Writing a business plan: www.gov.uk/write-business-plan – includes downloadable templates as well as advice.

Support for small businesses: www.gov.uk/browse/business

IPSE (The Association of Independent Professionals and the Self Employed) is a membership organisation giving support in a range of areas to freelances: www.ipse.co.uk

AIPP (Association of Independent Publishing Professionals) was founded in 2016 to support freelances working with indie authors and small publishing houses: www.aipponline.org

Louise Harnby: *Business Planning for Editorial Freelancers* www.louiseharnbyproofreader.com/business-planning-for-editorial-freelancers-a-guide-for-new-starters.html

Find your local chamber of commerce: www.britishchambers.org.uk

Planning for dealing with your death while still a practising editor or proofreader: http://blog.sfep.org.uk/succession-planning-for-your-business-after-you-die

This may also be of interest, a 2016 independent report on self-employment commissioned by the government:

www.gov.uk/government/uploads/system/uploads/attachment_data/file/
529702/ind-16-2-self-employment-review.pdf

SfEP

SfEP website: www.sfep.org.uk

For SfEP members:

Editing Matters archive: www.sfep.org.uk/resources/editing-matters

Editing Matters index: www.sfep.org.uk/resources/editing-matters/index

The range of forums: https://forums.sfep.org.uk/index.php

Ergonomic furniture, mice and keyboards

www.officefurnitureonline.co.uk/office-chairs/humanscale-seating

www.healthyworkstations.com

www.posturite.co.uk/ergonomic-mice-keyboards/ergonomic-keyboards.html

www.ergonomics.co.uk

Preventing workplace injury

Denise Cowle recommends these sites:

For a fuller explanation of RSI: www.nhs.uk/conditions/Repetitive-strain-injury/
Pages/Introduction.aspx

On back pain at work: www.nhs.uk/Livewell/workplacehealth/Pages/
backpainatwork.aspx

How to sit correctly: www.nhs.uk/Livewell/workplacehealth/Pages/
howtositcorrectly.aspx

Laptop health: www.nhs.uk/Livewell/workplacehealth/Pages/laptophealth.aspx

Common posture mistakes and fixes: www.nhs.uk/Livewell/Backpain/Pages/
back-pain-and-common-posture-mistakes.aspx

Tax and national insurance, VAT etc.

At the time of this Guide going to press, HMRC was beta-testing a new site for its internal manual. This affects URLs given here that begin 'www.gov.uk/ hmrc-internal-manuals/business-income-manual'. The latest versions available at the time are given, but note that some links may break – in which case, put the introductory phrase given here for the URL into the webpage's search function.

HMRC key help

www.gov.uk/government/collections/hmrc-webinars-email-alerts-and-videos

HMRC YouTube channel: www.youtube.com/user/HMRCgovuk

Tax help factsheets: www.gov.uk/government/collections/hm-revenue-and-customs-leaflets-factsheets-and-booklets

HMRC how to contact us: www.gov.uk/contact-hmrc

Sign up for free email help: https://public-online.hmrc.gov.uk/business-emails/subscription

Newly self-employed helpline: 0300 200 3504

VAT helpline: 0300 200 3700

Self-employment and HMRC – getting started

Running a business from home: www.gov.uk/run-business-from-home

How to register with HMRC: www.gov.uk/new-business-register-for-tax

Starting your own business: www.hmrc.gov.uk/courses/SYOB3/syob_3/html/syob_3_menu.html

Self-employed and claiming Working Tax Credit: www.gov.uk/government/publications/revenue-and-customs-brief-7-2015-new-rules-for-the-self-employed-claiming-working-tax-credit

Business expenses

Allowable professional subscriptions (aka 'List 3'): www.gov.uk/government/publications/professional-bodies-approved-for-tax-relief-list-3

Capital or revenue? www.gov.uk/hmrc-internal-manuals/business-income-manual/bim35000

What is and isn't allowable? www.gov.uk/hmrc-internal-manuals/business-income-manual/bim42526

More info on 'cost of sales' (HS222): www.gov.uk/government/publications/how-to-calculate-your-taxable-profits-hs222-self-assessment-helpsheet

Simplified expenses: www.gov.uk/simpler-income-tax-simplified-expenses

What does 'wholly and exclusively' mean? www.gov.uk/hmrc-internal-manuals/business-income-manual/bim42105

Travel & subsistence information: www.gov.uk/hmrc-internal-manuals/business-income-manual/bim47705

Calculating your tax and NICs liability

How to calculate your taxable profit: www.gov.uk/government/publications/how-to-calculate-your-taxable-profits-hs222-self-assessment-helpsheet

How to get your SA302 tax calculation: www.gov.uk/sa302-tax-calculation

Tax allowances and reliefs: www.gov.uk/expenses-if-youre-self-employed

Current tax and NI rates: www.gov.uk/government/collections/rates-and-allowances-hm-revenue-and-customs

Changes to collection of Class 2 NICs: www.gov.uk/government/publications/class-2-national-insurance-contributions

Ready reckoner: www.gov.uk/self-assessment-ready-reckoner

Keeping your pay and tax records for Self-Assessment

www.gov.uk/keeping-your-pay-tax-records/overview

Info on record-keeping: www.gov.uk/self-employed-records

Paper self-employment page: www.gov.uk/government/uploads/system/uploads/attachment_data/file/501544/sa103f-2016.pdf

Keeping VAT records: www.gov.uk/vat-record-keeping

Mobile record-keeping apps

www.gov.uk/government/publications/record-keeping-and-simpler-income-tax-applicationssoftware

Info on mobile apps: www.gov.uk/government/collections/record-keeping-and-simpler-income-tax-applicationssoftware and www.gov.uk/government/news/mobile-apps

Use of home as office

Tax relief for use of home for business: www.gov.uk/hmrc-internal-manuals/business-income-manual/bim47825

www.gov.uk/hmrc-internal-manuals/business-income-manual/bim47805

Valuation Office Agency advice on working from home and council tax: www.gov.uk/introduction-to-business-rates/working-at-home

Invoicing and pursuing payment

Content of invoices

www.gov.uk/invoicing-and-taking-payment-from-customers/invoices-what-they-must-include

Charging interest on late payment

www.gov.uk/late-commercial-payments-interest-debt-recovery/charging-interest-commercial-debt

Marketing

SfEP Guide: Sara Hulse, *Marketing Yourself: Strategies to promote your editorial business*, 2nd edition.

SfEP suggested minimum rates: www.sfep.org.uk/resources/suggested-minimum-rates

Louise Harnby, *Marketing Your Editing & Proofreading Business*
www.louiseharnbyproofreader.com/marketing-your-editing--proofreading-business.html

The law on marketing and advertising

www.gov.uk/marketing-advertising-law

Cold-calling advice

www.theguardian.com/small-business-network/2016/jan/07/introverts-succeed-sales-prepation-cold-calling

Planning and time management

Tracking your time

https://toggl.com

http://tomato-timer.com

www.freshbooks.com (an accounting package with a built-in time tracker)

www.getharvest.com

www.intuit.co.uk

www.blueskyapp.com (an accounting app with a built-in time tracker)

www.timestamp.io

http://slimtimer.com

http://timesheet.rauscha.com

www.hourstrackerapp.com (iPhone and Android)

www.thrivesolo.com

www.zoho.com/uk/invoice (an accounting solution with time tracker)

www.getklok.com

www.dualitysoft.com/dsclock

https://pro.trackingtime.co

To help you keep focused

https://freedom.to

www.proginosko.com/leechblock

http://focusme.co/features

https://chrome.google.com/webstore/detail/stayfocusd/laankejkbhbdhmipfmgcngdelahlfoji

https://selfcontrolapp.com (for Macs)

To remind you to take breaks

A review of several apps: www.umsystem.edu/totalrewards/wellness/activity_and_break_apps

Non-distracting background sounds

www.noisli.com and www.youtube.com/watch?v=eKFTSSKCzWA

Skills and knowledge

The National Occupational Standards (2012) for the publishing arena: www.publishingtrainingcentre.co.uk/images/BookJournalPublishingNationalStandards.pdf

Courses from the SfEP: www.sfep.org.uk/training/choose-a-course

Courses from the Publishing Training Centre: www.publishingtrainingcentre.co.uk

Proofreading PDFs: https://bookmachine.org/2015/12/07/pdf-proofreading-essential-first-step-checks

Stamps of BSI symbols for marking up PDFs are available from Claire Ruben: www.faircopy.co.uk/downloads.html
and from Louise Harnby: www.louiseharnbyproofreader.com/blog-the-proofreaders-parlour/roundup-pdf-proofreading-stamps-quick-access-links

The SfEP range of guides: www.sfep.org.uk/resources/guides

The Editorial Freelance Association (US) range of guides: www.lulu.com/spotlight/editorialfreelancers

Places to ask peers questions

For SfEP members, the SfEP forums, of course: https://forums.sfep.org.uk/index.php

And, if you choose wisely, www.facebook.com. Facebook groups to consider joining include the SfEP (www.facebook.com/EditProof); The Unofficial SfEP; Editors' Association of Earth (EAE); EAE Backroom (a closed group, where your questions and comments won't be indexed so won't pop up to embarrass you in browser searches); Conferences for Editors; EAE Ad Space; Academic Editors; Fiction Writers and Editors; and Certifications for Copyeditors, for starters.

Editorial tools

Paul Beverley's macros: www.archivepub.co.uk/macros.html

Jack Lyons' book on Word for editors: www.editorium.com/msword4pubpros.htm

Editorium: www.editorium.com (for the Editor's Toolkit and more)

Kutools: www.extendoffice.com/product/kutools-for-word.html

Mike's Toolbox: http://mikestoolbox.weebly.com

PerfectIt: www.intelligentediting.com (PC only)

ReferenceChecker: www.goodcitations.com (32-bit Word only)

WordTips for wrangling Word: http://word.tips.net for Word 97 to 2003 and http://wordribbon.tips.net for Word 2007 onwards

Text expanders can help if you find you're typing the same query over and over – in effect, a sophisticated version of autocompletion. Some of these can be found at:
www.16software.com/breevy
https://textexpander.com
www.nch.com.au/fastfox
www.phraseexpress.com

Computer tech

To enable your Mac to run Windows programs: www.parallels.com/uk

John Espirian's blog: http://espirian.co.uk/blog is a great source for tech help and ideas, especially for Mac users. He is on Vimeo, too: https://vimeo.com/espirian

References

1. www.gov.uk/write-business-plan

2. www.sfep.org.uk/training/mentoring

3. www.amazon.co.uk/?ie=UTF8&link_code=hom&tag=societyforedi-21

4. www.sfep.org.uk/resources/editing-matters

5. https://en.wikipedia.org/wiki/List_of_style_guides#General

6. www.buzzfeed.com/emmyf/buzzfeed-style-guide

7. www.asd-ste100.org

8. www.scientificstyleandformat.org/Home.html

9. www.thebookseller.com

10. http://publishingperspectives.com

11. https://forums.sfep.org.uk/index.php

12. www.sfep.org.uk/networking/local

13. www.kokedit.com/ckb.php

14. www.gov.uk/plan-retirement-income/overview

15. www.gov.uk/government/uploads/system/uploads/attachment_data/file/ 514268/self-employment-and-the_state-pension-apr-2016.pdf

16. www.gov.uk/working-for-yourself/what-counts-as-self-employed

17. www.gov.uk/set-up-sole-trader/register

18. www.gov.uk/browse/business

19. www.gov.uk/government/collections/hmrc-webinars-email-alerts-and-videos

20. www.gov.uk/capital-allowances

21. www.hmrc.gov.uk/courses/SYOB3/syob_3_exps/html/syob_3_exps_menu.html

22. www.gov.uk/expenses-if-youre-self-employed

23. www.gov.uk/government/news/webinars-and-videos-about-self-assessment

24. www.gov.uk/vat-registration

25. www.gov.uk/government/publications/vat-notice-7001-should-i-be-registered-for-vat/vat-notice-7001-should-i-be-registered-for-vat

26. www.gov.uk/government/uploads/system/uploads/attachment_data/file/501544/sa103f-2016.pdf

27. http://tools.hmrc.gov.uk/hmrctaxcalculator/screen/Personal+Tax+Calculator/en-GB/summary?user=guest (If the site gives an error message, click on the Restart the Tax Calculator link.)

28. www.gov.uk/invoicing-and-taking-payment-from-customers/invoices-what-they-must-include

29. www.gov.uk/late-commercial-payments-interest-debt-recovery/charging-interest-commercial-debt

30. www.paypal.com/uk/webapps/mpp/home

31. www.writersandartists.co.uk/listings

32. www.sfep.org.uk/members/getting-work/directory (In the members' area)

33. www.sfep.org.uk/members/getting-work/im-available (In the members' area)

34. www.sfep.org.uk/members/benefits/freelancers-in-the-uk (In the members' area)

35. Locate your local chamber at www.britishchambers.org.uk

36. One such thread is: https://forums.sfep.org.uk/read.php?2,74806 (In the members' area)

37. www.freelanceuk.com/technology/advice_register_domain_name.shtml

38. www.gov.uk/marketing-advertising-law/direct-marketing

39. www.sfep.org.uk/resources/suggested-minimum-rates

40. www.sfep.org.uk/members/pay-rates-and-pay-problems/rate-for-the-job-intro (In the members' area)

41. https://americaneditor.wordpress.com

42. www.louiseharnbyproofreader.com/blog-the-proofreaders-parlour/editorial-annual-accounts-template-excel

43. www.year-planner-calendar.co.uk/year-planner-wall-diary-calendar-public-holiday-chart-academic-fiscal-free.htm

44. www.sfep.org.uk/standards/code-of-practice

45. www.sfep.org.uk/resources/top-tips

46. www.sfep.org.uk/standards/contracts/model-terms-and-conditions

47. www.sfep.org.uk/members/benefits/legal-help (In the members' area)

48. Such as www.youtube.com/watch?v=ZwobgUP9ijU

49. www.denisecowleeditorial.com/blog/in-summary-sit-less-stand-more-stretch-often

50. https://forums.sfep.org.uk/read.php?2,82707,82707#msg-82707 (In the members' area)

51. https://forums.sfep.org.uk/read.php?13,97000,97000#msg-97000 (In the members' area)

52. www.sfep.org.uk/members/governance-and-management/membership-map (In the members' area)

53. The World Health Organization defined wellness thus in its 1946 constitution (my emphasis): 'Health is a state of complete physical, mental *and social well-being* and not merely the absence of disease or infirmity.'

54. https://support.microsoft.com/en-us/help/17128/windows-8-file-history

55. https://support.apple.com/en-gb/HT201250

56. www.policybee.co.uk

57. www.sfep.org.uk/members/benefits/professional-indemnity-insurance (In the members' area)

58. www.hiscox.co.uk/business-insurance/professional-indemnity-insurance

59. www.caunceohara.co.uk

60. www.bluefingroup.co.uk

61. www.sfep.org.uk/membership/benefits